T0208712

Parental Alienation Syndrome and Me

David Goodman

Parental Alienation Syndrome and Me
One Father's Story and Poems

iUniverse books may be ordered through booksellers or by contacting:

iUniverse
1663 Liberty Drive
Bloomington, IN 47403
www.iuniverse.com
1-800-Authors (1-800-288-4677)

Because of the dynamic nature of the Internet, any Web addresses or links contained in this book may have changed since publication and may no longer be valid. The views expressed in this work are solely those of the author and do not necessarily reflect the views of the publisher, and the publisher hereby disclaims any responsibility for them.

ISBN: 978-1-4502-6412-9 (sc)
ISBN: 978-1-4502-6414-3 (e)

Print information available on the last page.

iUniverse rev. date: 09/21/2018

Contents

Introduction

My name is David. Like most, I was born gasping for air and screaming. My family tells me that I was a cute kid, with lots of blond curls and chubby cheeks. Later I learned to ride a bike and graduated from high school and college. I loved sports and music, fell in love with women, broke a few hearts, had my heart broken, and became an adult—slowly. I thought about life and death, and I laughed a lot.

Pretty normal, huh? So, why write a book? you might ask.

The answer? Because the worst thing that could happen to someone happened to me. After you read this book, the story, select your favorite poem, and see the truth-telling pictures drawn by a child's own hand, will you agree?

What made this the worst thing that could happen was that it began as the best thing—I became a father. I realized I loved someone much more than myself, more than life itself. This love for your child *is* life, the ultimate gift, the ultimate life. Parents know this so well. Once you have a child, everything changes—forever.

My story will explain what parental alienation (PA) is, and how brainwashing isn't just advertising genius or some government turning people into sheep. My story will tell you how, for over a decade, I had a happy, loving relationship with my daughter, and then, in one weekend, she vanished. My story may awaken your consciousness. I hope it does.

My name is still David. However, when my daughter was a toddler, one of my names was Tickle Monster. That's the name I made up to go along with one of our favorite pastimes. I would get on the floor with my daughter and tickle her, making her squeal in delight and yell for mercy. No matter how long our day, or how many days since we had seen each other, we would come to the apartment and, even before snacks, throw ourselves down on the carpet, and I would become the Walt Disney monster of tickle.

First I'd tickle away at her feet and the sides of the belly, hearing loud screams of excitement and thrill. Then Fart Monster would arrive, that blowing on the skin monster that makes the funny noise that no one can resist laughing at, and then back to Tickle Monster and little Pinch Monster, too. Then back to Tickle Monster, going for the lose-control areas—full belly and underarms! After a few moments of even wilder screams, my daughter would lower her voice and, in a gasp for air, say, "Stop, Daddy, stop." I'd get scared and stop. Then she'd say, with a twinkle in her eye, "Do it again! Do it again!" She had me wrapped around her little finger—for life.

This is how my daughter and I started: innocent, one with each other and life. We were from the heart with communication and love.

We have no communication now. Our love is beaten to death. Her subconscious has no memory of us except a hatred of me.

Why?

Parental alienation.

The Kiss in the Cave

When I was young, there were television shows that scared the hell out of me. I know there were only four main stations, and all were in black and white, so how much damage could they do? What could be so scary on television that I'd be writing about it almost a half century later? What played in the psyche so strong that it could convince a young boy alone at night to be scared of life? What?

I'll tell you.

It wasn't the movie *Psycho*. It wasn't the nearly two hundred *Twilight Zone* episodes. It was one simple movie: *The Invasion of the Body Snatchers*. A 1950s film about a man in a California hospital with large, terror-filled eyes, who was sweating profusely and screaming, "You've got to stop them! You've got to stop them!" I guess he's in the psych ward. It's a dramatic scene that is gripping and eye-opening. The panicked man finally settles down and tells the whole story. There are always two sides to a story.

He explains in detail how, in his small town, pods the size of human beings end up near each person; when a person falls asleep, the pod becomes them, looks like them. The big difference, however, is the pod doesn't have their heart and soul. Aliens from outer space take over humans one at a time. *All you have to do is go to sleep.*

The scene that took me over the edge was when the doctor from that small town (that same hysterical man in the hospital) ran into a cave with his girlfriend. Both were frightened and exhausted from staying up all night. The doctor screams her name and yells, "Don't sleep! Don't sleep!" He kisses her a desperate, loving kiss on the lips. Too late. Her haunting and distant eyes open, and she looks straight at the doctor and says, "Don't fight it. It's wonderful. You can't escape it."

I'll never forget her eyes.

I'll never forget the change.

I'll never forget her leaving him.

At the end of the movie, the hospitalized doctor starts to flip out again and is screaming, "Stop them! Stop them!"

The authorities and men in white coats say, "Put him away."

Then, all of a sudden, there is a conversation with a newly arrived policeman who says a whole trailer of pods spilled over on the highway.

It's clear now, the story the small town doctor told was true. Life can be scary, and it can happen to you.

Love Is Good—Still

Dropping you at school was our last
Day together

Love doesn't remember
Another

Today is the same day
Although it's not my way

Hey I can still say
I love you TODAY!!!

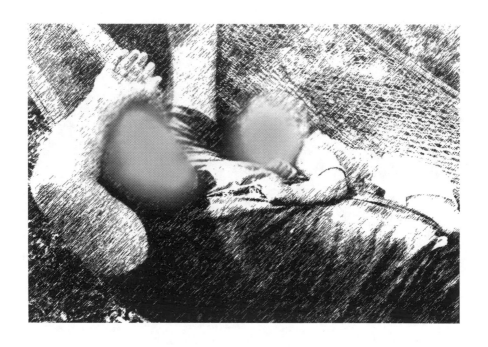

PAS

Parental alienation occurs when one parent successfully manipulates a child (children) to turn against the other parent. PAS (Parental Alienation Syndrome) was identified by psychiatrist, researcher, and child advocate Dr. Richard Gardner in the 1980s.

Why did I change the subject from *The Invasion of the Body Snatchers* to PAS? The effect is the same. Children are taken over, brainwashed.

With children you can see their eyes wide open to life and their loving hearts made of gold. You love your children. They are your world. You love them more than life. In fact, they are all about life, the most beautiful presence of life in the universe and the most special of all to our hearts.

Their simple smiles.

Their laughter.

Their faces.

Their shiny hair and rosy cheeks.

You stare at them when they sleep. The silence then is an eternal, all-encompassing look at life itself.

Your heart breaks when they get sick.

You never, ever stop thinking about them. They are always in your subconscious. You dream all the time about them. You dream big dreams of growing older with them and of when they get married and who their spouse will be. The biggest dream of all—their children. You wonder what it will feel like when you hold their children. One day your dream will happen, the kiss of life.

Perhaps you dream of dancing at their wedding. Perhaps you dream backward—first steps, first fall, first training-wheeled bike ride with you running behind.

When you become a parent, everything changes forever.

The first time your child becomes very sick, you call to God, atheist or not. With fortune, God arrives just in time and the illness passes and you are eternally connected to the universe and your heart. Praise God.

So, how does a sci-fi story and PAS connect? They are both inside jobs. You can call it brainwashing. You can call it impossible. Children in America and all over the world lose one of their parents. Children go to sleep, emotionally and mentally. One parent is the alienating parent, and the other parent (who will lose the child) is the targeted parent. No movie. No pods.

This can happen in twenty-four hours.

It happened to me.

I Know You Can't See Me

I know you can't see me
I'm standing behind you.

You see my shadow
In front of you.

You hate my shadow
And you want it to go.

There's a lot you don't know
And the shadow won't go.

Turn around, Baby
I love you so!

Devastation

Devastation is the word I use even though there has to be a word bigger and stronger. How do I tell someone I lost my child? Did I drive off and leave her at the gas station? Where did she go? Was she killed? Can she be found?

Heck, she might be living down the block from you. You might be still talking to her mother. You might be mowing her mother's yard. You may have processed the months and months, turning into years and years, of child support payments that I sent in while you sat warm and safe in your cubicle. As the years rolled by, and I couldn't see or talk to my child, who was responsible? Would someone do this deliberately? For what reason? For what gain? By what means, deceit?

When children are gone, life's precious moments dig deep into the heart, ripping out each day, each moment, each thought. Breath by breath. Each cell in the body, the trillion times a trillion, gasps for fresh air like fish flopping on the ground. Each cell is completely devastated. Each cell remembers. Each cell is starving for that last look into your darling's eyes: that look of innocence, that presence of the universe and God, that strong bond and connection, that one thing on earth that keeps our species thriving. Yes, this human biology is a salient warmth and love that lasts forever. It's like a Mona Lisa smile, the smile that wins over devastation.

So why are children being stolen and brainwashed? Because a parent can. Of the couples that divorce and experience PAS, it's an equal opportunity for women or men to become alienators. The parental percentages don't matter. What does matter: 100 percent of the affected children are victims. All alienated children are victims of PAS unless a parent's offense against the child is heinous and proven so. It should never be that the alienating parent gets away with their own bias. Why can the alienating parent act as judge, as God?

But back to devastation.

David Goldman's ex-wife, Bruna Bianchi Carneiro Ribeiro, took their then four-year-old son to Brazil. Bruna passed away while out of the country, and David fought for five years to be reunited with his son, Sean. As David said on television in June of 2009, "It's beyond cruel." The US government encouraged Brazil to reunite the son with his father. This occurred on Christmas Eve 2009, with Sean and David returning to the United States to begin their healing.

Words can't explain the loss of a child. Maybe our last picture can. My daughter and I look happy. Baggy clothes. Dark colors. She's tall with dark brown hair. I'm wearing the stupid black baseball hat she gave me for my birthday. We both have the same wide smile. Then there's one beautiful unseen thing. It's small and unimportant—maybe. But it's huge. In the moment of the picture, my daughter puts her hand behind her back and holds my hand. It's such a simple, honest touch. Such a true sign of love in front of the camera's eye. She was still a preteen.

Devastation? Way beyond devastation for our two souls. Every cell in two people calls to each other.

You might not believe this, but please think about it. If "slices" of different hearts are put together beating their individual electrical pulses, in a small amount of time they'll be beating alike. Can you imagine the same cells, DNA, blood, thoughts, hearts being apart yet together?

They say you know you have a heart when you have a child because the heart is pulled from your chest and walks the earth.

Devastation? Way beyond ... way, way beyond. You should have seen the look on my best friend's face when I said, "If this had happened when my daughter was five or six years old, I couldn't have taken it. I may have checked out." He looked at me like I was nuts.

The child is devastated unconsciously, dormant inside himself or herself. The parent is devastated consciously, every second of their life.

I know it's all about the child. This is devastating to the child, who later can act out using sex, emotions, feelings, drugs, relationships, male bashing, female bashing, loss of faith, perhaps loss of God. Children are damaged from the inside out. Taken. Wouldn't it be terrible to falsely hate your father, spending the rest of your life hating boyfriends and husbands? That's what can happen. This abuse during childhood definitely remains subconscious and grows into adulthood along with the victim. There are good PAS books out there. True stories. True studies. Check the web. Check your heart. Check with life. Check with God. It's important to see both sides of any story.

Parents and society are trying to save their children's lives by undoing and waking them up from possibly the most horrific wrong to life: turning the child against his or her own parent because one parent hates the other parent or is selfish. My hope is that all alienated children wake up, including mine.

Nuclear Bomb—In My Closet

Was it accident
Was it destiny
An unknown closet
Centered in my house of me.

Of me, of me
My child buried alive
Not known, you see.

Ten years gone
Friends and family too
Now I hold the master
Key.

The closet is open …
It stinks of some modern-day mothers
    Or fathers
With knapsack nuclear bombs

Sipping tea

Sipping tea.

Freud Said

Freud said something like, there's nothing in this world as hard to do as parenting. Parenting is a wonderful world. When you have your first child, it wakes you up, it changes you forever. It's truly the spring of life. Love and joy are in abundance. Your whole life is about your new child: sharing the baby with relatives, playing, protecting, feeding, changing diapers, buying new clothes, holding, and rocking, as well as making lots of foolish-looking baby faces to light up your child's smile. Parents are in their own world of love and adoration for the new baby. It will last a lifetime unless PAS comes knocking on your door.

Everyone knows that parents will get upset, angry, and possibly violent if you do something wrong to their child. Society tries to protect its children against threats such as stranger danger, drugs, child molesters, cults, and evil indoctrinations.

I know there are a lot of gray areas. I know there is even evil pretending to be good. I know people dig in hard and deep because they believe they are right. The ego is at stake. The self-righteous, all-encompassing, obsessed, controlling ego. That Parent ego can convince an alienating parent that, because they love their child so much, anything is justifiable—any method, any indoctrination, any end result by any means necessary, including their own acts amounting to child abuse.

The big problem with children being brainwashed by one parent against the other is that children don't know they are brainwashed. One parent is successfully manipulating the child or children using money, power, guilt, and/or pressure to succumb to their will.* When extreme, this is called Stockholm Syndrome (a sister of Parental Alienation Syndrome), a deep, unconscious fear of the dominant person that results in siding with that person for survival and safety.

Nothing becomes perfectly clear until the opposite is seen. It's only when one sees the other side of the story that one wakes up. That's why cults and brainwashing are so difficult to reverse and the loss of a child to them is the ultimate hate crime in America.

There are three types of PAS: mild, moderate, and severe. Unfortunately, mine is severe. I have not seen or talked to my daughter since she was a preteen. She went through junior high, high school, and college as if I died. However, I've been here the entire time, sending cards, presents, happy notes and letters, and childhood home movies. My therapist even wrote her a letter pleading for her to hear the truth, not just half the truth. Brainwashing doesn't allow openness or dialogue. Brainwashing is about "all or nothing." Brainwashing is about one parent winning, and the winner takes all. In my case, that meant taking my daughter.

*PAS may happen to only one child in a household of multiple children or to any combination of those youngsters.

No More Wire Hangers

No more wire hangers said Joan
No more You can't handle the truth! said Jack
No more father to remember
No more danger, danger
Or moan

Mom's in control now
Everything is going to be great
Mom's the good fairy white
Glowing with a
Bow

The cards have been reshuffled
The deck's been cut
I've changed my first and last name
{His heart muffled}
A lot

Mom and Dad are done, it's officially a bust
Everything's perfect now
Except this wire hanger

With rust

With rust

Mirror in Front of the Couch

Gail came into my life when I sat down on the couch in front of her nearly a decade ago. Years had gone by without me starting therapy or taking antidepressant drugs or joining a support group. There was no one to turn to before PAS was known to me. This was when I was in the closet of hell—without my child, with a billion gallons of tears usually released Sunday afternoons. Gail said that was the time I was most alone; when life looked at itself; where time stood still; where the week of worry, self-pity, sleeplessness, nightmares, and fear of never seeing my daughter again revealed itself. Sundays. The horror.

Can you imagine your child *gone*? Taken by a motorcycle gang or a crazy man with tattoos and missing teeth or a good-looking man in a suit with perfect hair and a manicure? No clues. Just GONE.

Perhaps she is gone with a favorite trusted family member. Maybe she's gone when you turned your back for two seconds. It can happen. You never suspect this from a person you used to love and respect. Your co-parent. The person you cherished simply because they were the other parent of your beloved child.

Anyway, back to Gail. As I sat in front of her, I noticed she was a lovely woman, with a halo of beautiful brown hair, and that she sat upright and looked directly at me. My words jumped out at her immediately. I said, "I don't want therapy. I just want a strategy to get my daughter back." Then I started on my story. At a certain point in my narration, Gail said flatly, "They'd have to lock me up if they took my children." Inside me I felt God, the universe, and children became one at that moment. My own therapist would go nuts. Of course she would. It's a normal human reaction when it comes to our children that we love so dearly. At last, validation.

Gail probably said three or four hundred words to me in ten years (or so it seemed). That's because I talked so much and she listened, allowing the grief to come out of me. How else could I have let go of the human disaster, the ultimate hurt as a human being? She prayed and prayed for me and my daughter. She's praying now.

Depression

It's like a black dog
In a white ice cave

The black head is down
The cold is not felt

It's just a picture in the head
Like the day we did wed

A silent picture
Nothing is said

Friends and family and society
Dead

They know and understand
And are very well read

They look at that black dog
And know it is me

This is all of life
And it's me that they
See

But I am sad
For God said
Forgive them for they know
Not what they do …

You see, God lost his child, too

Be glad it didn't happen to you

But it did

Henry David Thoreau

Every once in a while, someone says something to you that gets you going. I was at KU, twenty-two years old, when my English teacher said, "If you read one book in your life, read *Walden* by Henry David Thoreau." The teacher had my attention because not once, but twice, he apologized to me in front of the class for spilling beer on my paper while grading at home. As I was also studying statistics in biology class, I knew that to spill beer on only my paper when there were over fifty students in the class, and to do it twice, was statistically an anomaly.

What's important at this point is that fate acted upon me. Each page I turned in *Walden* was special. What a genius Thoreau was. A genius about life, independence, self-reliance, time, the absence of time, character, dignity, government, the absence of government, racism, health, dreaming your dreams, and putting a foundation under those dreams. There was a heart and a soul to that book. He had two hundred books printed. He never saw them sold or the enormous success that would blow in the winds of the future.

So what's he got to do with my daughter? With children? With children that are brainwashed? With children with severe PAS that decide to never talk to or see the targeted parent? Not much except that Thoreau was the opposite. He sat alone and lived life in the free. He knew all the colors of man were of no concern. He'd walk twenty miles to keep a winter's sunshine view of a special tree with fresh white snow and a blue jay eating a red berry. He knew nature was where we are from and what we still are despite governments, false religions, and mankind's brainwashing. He didn't buy society's hypocritical morality and injustice. His God wasn't about materialism and selfishness. Life wasn't something to use for manipulating another human being. Life is God's energy in us, enough energy to love a Mom and a Dad.

Now the opposite of Thoreau would be the two Kims that have ruled North Korea (Kim Jong Il and his son Kim Jong Un). Under their dictatorship, two- to four-year-old children are sent (made to go) to school and are brainwashed to adore everything about the Kims' life, government, and character in a totalitarian way. Get them while they are young! Except it's not God, Walt

Disney, or the tooth fairy. The very young children's psyches, love, and respect of life itself are turned over to these two idiots. To punish, torture, steal, and rape life at the beginning of childhood is a crime, a grandiose national hate crime.

Brainwashers of life and children are everywhere, from Hitler to the animated movie *Animal Farm*. That classic tale depicts those in control as the storytellers, allowing them to write and rewrite history This rewriting frames our thoughts and how we see who we are—in effect, remapping our brains. The human brain changes and grows and develops until we are twenty-four to twenty-five years old. Brainwashing is everywhere and it pays off, just ask advertisers of television and print ads. There are no pods; we just show up with our credit cards. Be careful who you give your life to; it is precious and full of love, respect, and kindness. The real story of life only comes to children's consciousness when they see their parents for who they are: Two people who fell in love, wanted children, wanted to love them, and made the promise that the children would be the most important beings in the whole wide world to them. Two people who wanted to love their children but were far from perfect, far from being free of vices, not given any real training in proper parenting before their children were born. Two people who winged it.

Obsessive control (fear) by one parent against the other convinces the alienated child that one parent is all good and the targeted parent is all bad—an act of cruelty to the child and the human spirit. It's like the young human spirit is a plant that seeks to survive, bask in the sunlight, and grow. Have you not seen a plant grow sideways or bend or reach to catch the healthy rays of the sun? Children want to know the truth. They want to love both of their parents. However, one parent got hold of the light switch, turning the lights off. That switch is turned back on an average of twenty years later by the adult child victim of parental alienation when they realize what the one (alienating) parent has done to them. This is a long time for a lesson in life. It's a long time to wait to see Mommy or Daddy again.

Humans know there are two sides to every story; however, it's just too painful or obtuse after being brainwashed. Whether in your dreams or your subconscious or maybe deep in your heart, there is a candle of light reflecting truth. The truth never goes away, and the truth shall set you free!

A Thought ...
Never Mind

A thought of ten thousand,
Oh daughter of mine.

How I may
Show and convince
I am kind.

No such luck
I can find.
But one last thought.

Is it art, is it poetry?
It can!
It can! It can!

"I say I love you,
You're mine!"

Please, sweetheart, awake.
It's me in you
You find.

Me

I thought it was normal to be beaten severely by Grandmother, Mom, and my stepfather. Not really. But I knew other kids back then who were also beaten. This is a list of what I was hit with: switches, shoes, wire hangers, belts (the metal belt buckles were the worst), sticks, flyswatters, rulers (which broke easily), and the reliable hand. There were plenty of hand swats.

When you can talk about something, it's a good thing. It's the stuff you can't or don't say that's dangerous. Words can be very healing. It's those dark, deep feelings we protect in our heart that get us. That's what makes saying and receiving "I am sorry" and "I love you" so powerful.

Growing up I moved well over fifty times; attended eighteen different schools; taught myself my ABCs at the end of second grade (later I learned that I had a learning disability); was poor; went to Baptist churches and Catholic masses; and was very grateful that I wasn't drafted to fight in Vietnam.

Yep, that's my childhood. That's me. But I never dreamed something *really* bad would happen to me until I lost my only child, my heart, my soul, my everything.

There is only one hurt in my heart, the first and only hurt: my daughter has been brainwashed. Combined with the brainwashing is the fact that her inner child has never had a chance to escape (Stockholm Syndrome), never had a chance to defend *her* feelings or *her* daddy, never had a chance to truly hear the other side of the story. Nor could she understand what one parent was willing to do to become the only parent, the so-called good parent, the so-called right parent, the deceiving owner of my daughter's soul.

Once PAS started, my calls with my daughter were through. She was pretty numb and impersonal, only answering mundane questions with a simple yes or no. However, about a month into PAS, she answered my phone voice with: "Hi, Dad!" The real feelings came out. So long ago, yet this is what I hold on to.

For years she wore the watch I gave her, into which I had programmed family phone numbers and emergency contacts.

She told my brother he had more hair than me. Was that a put-down, or was her subconscious speaking and thinking about me?

This is something I wish she could hear from me: honey, I never went away from you. For years I called at the appointed time, the only time allotted me. I sent you plenty of cards and presents, which you never got. When you became a teenager, I waited for you to be through with high school because I knew for sure, I was so positive, that you'd want me in your life. That was, however, before I learned about PAS. I didn't know about Dr. Richard Gardner. The books about PAS were yet to come. The truth can't be stopped now.

Living Conditions

My house is studio
My mattress is air
My van is '96
My Home Depot table is desk
And will do.

Hot oatmeal for breakfast
Fried rice for dinner,
Old socks and no animals,
Winter of life
Not past.

Writing at 3:00 AM
Staring at the wall,
It's the most important
Thing in life I love
My darling daughter,
I call.

These four hand-drawn pictures and writing are by my daughter and say it all about the child's view of PAS. Can you see her brainwashing (PAS) fear?

This is what one of my families looks like all together...

This is what one of my families looks like all together...

When I was very little, I looked like this.

Myself

This is what I look like when I'm happy.

This is what I look like when I'm sad.

This is what I look like when I am bard.

I like myself because I live.

Sometimes I don't like myself because my mom yells at me.

My Favorite Kid!

When my child was little, four to about ten years old, I would tease, "You're my favorite kid," and she'd say with attitude, "Daddy, I'm your only kid," and I'd say, "I know, but you're still my favorite kid." When she stopped having a twinkle in her eye, I stopped saying that stupid joke.

Another joke, among the many: "Don't forget, I am the meanest Daddy in the whole wide world." She would look cross at me and say, "No! The nicest!" A co-worker of mine used to say this to his kids, and for some reason I started saying it, too, just to get the love to ooze out.

You know, in my wildest dreams or nightmares, never would I have thought a person could do this to another parent, let alone a child. Even though Arkansas hosts a Parental Alienation Syndrome Day, and some states have a parent go to jail for stopping visitation rights, society and the legal system have let our children down. The pain, the suffering, and the alienation continue. Through the PAS websites, books, and consciousness raising, may the light of God be seen and the kiss of truth be felt by every parent, family member, friend of families, and every decent person who realizes children of PAS are victims of child abuse, and may all people act on their good conscience knowing that God lives inside of us as well our precious children.

> I will never stop loving my child.
> When she does wake up from PAS, it will be sudden,
> A phone call, a letter, a shift of life.
> I will never lose faith.
> I will wait for her here on earth or in heaven.
> I will never not keep her in my heart.
> For right now, I wait.
>
> And miles to go before I sleep.
> And miles to go before I sleep.

It's Very Large, It's Very Small

It's very large, it's very small
The universe knows and it calls
Two is one and one is two
We're all connected in the
Dark-light whole.

The speed of light
The sound of love
Love connects the stars
Above.

It's very large, it's very small
When our eyes are closed
Burst colored brilliance
Of you and me, froze.

Walking barefoot on sea-shelled sand
Smiling hand in hand
It was but a dream on land
And a wide open door.

I sit and stare, and deep inside
I hold my breath
Close my eyes
And go right back …
For more.

Conclusion

A lifelong friend of mine kept saying to me, "They don't get it until it happens to them."

It took me a while, but finally, *I* got it. If parental alienation happened to you, you'd get it. If you are luckier than I, you are just living in a world where PA happens around you. Maybe it is happening to your friend, brother, sister, uncle, aunt, grandparents, co-worker, lover, nephew, niece, or new spouse. PA is on television, on the Internet, in the newspapers—it's everywhere.

Is PA the worst thing that could happen? If you had to sit in the back of the bus or hide your true sexuality or avoid going places where there is no ramp for your wheelchair, how would these life situations compare to your child or children being stolen from you?

There is an invisible killer of life out there. The loss of a child is a parent's worst nightmare ... every day.

If you're a child of Parental Alienation Syndrome, remember there are always two sides to each story. Information is available for you on the Internet and in books such as:

Adult Children of Parental Alienation Syndrome: Breaking the Ties that Bind, by Amy J. L. Baker (W. W. Norton & Company, New York, New York 10110, 2007)

A Family's Heartbreak: A Parent's Introduction to Parental Alienation, by Michael Jeffries, with Dr. Joel Davies (A Family's Heartbreak LLC, Stanford, CT, 2008)

Unlawful Flight: A Parental Kidnapping, by Glen C. Schulz (WindBlown Books, Houston, Texas 78414, 2007)

The truth of my story can be felt by all parents, and all parents-to-be, and all who love children.

Make injustice visible.
—Ghandi

THE LAST WORD

When a child of PAS becomes an adult and has not yet woken-up, it is because the verbal and non-verbal controls of the alienating parent are successful in the brainwashing and keeping the cult of two together against the targeted parent. This 'all good' parent against the 'all bad' parent is all that's needed combined with fear. The adult child of PAS has been in fear of the targeted parent for many years not knowing the truth, which would be revealed in hearing both sides of the story. This fear is a result of the alienating parent telling lies, half truths and the obsession to keep the targeted parent and family away. In the subconscious of the adult child of PAS is the real fear of the alienating parent. It is the fear of the force of the alienating parent that is angry, obsessive and controlling. If the child can't fight it, figure it out, or get away from it, then they become an innocent victim of PAS. That is child abuse.

Because the innocent child never had a chance to truly be with the targeted parent, hear their side of the story, ask questions, listen to answers, there was no chance for the targeted parent to defend themselves. This doesn't happen in the reality of morals . . . only in PAS.

In Amy J. L. Baker's book, **Adult Children of Parental Alienation Syndrome, Breaking the Ties that Bind**, there are eleven ways discussed how an adult child can wake-up to PAS. My favorite is maturation. You know, they just figure it out over time through understanding, intelligence and/or intuition. The unfortunate thing is that the research reveals that the average adult victim of PAS wakes up 20 years later. It hurts me to know that some will wake up down the road way too late for this short time we all have. All the healing could take place in the now.

For the child that is now an adult to wake-up, they need to be conscious of the painful truth. Therapy, trusting friends or a leap of faith may happen. Direct contact with the targeted parent immediately or slowly can be done. Eventually, the alienating parent will find out. They will huff and puff, but they will have to accept this. It is the adult child of PAS's right and destiny, with new consciousness, that was wrongfully repressed and is now free

It is so simple, but yet hard. The adult child of PAS is now awakened...

claiming maybe for the first time in their life: their childhood, their inner child, their maturity, independence in their life. Life that the alienating parent took from them.

And The Truth Shall Set You Free.

***In the study, all forty adult children of PAS said they wished the alienated parent would not give up on them.

More Poetry by David Goodman

One Thought Equals Eternity

One thought
One now
One decision
One God-like synapse

Nothing bought
Nothing but sour
Nothing of a son
Nothing father-daughter
But gaps

One thought
One life
One father-daughter

O God
Give us
The thought of life
A father-daughter love

The eternal maps

Touch

Touch
So old not new
Memory old

I let go
Not a clue

But when
I am touched
So accidentally
I remember all of me

So young
So innocent
My life on the take

Before the kiss
Before the make

Everlasting touch

All senses awake

My heart, my soul

Scream!

And then ache …

Onions on the Merry-Go-Round

The onions on the merry-go-round
Go around and around
And as I look over
My shoulder
The layers of onion
Come off
One by one

I look into the past
And I see the smile
In the onion say
Come on home

But I keep going
Round and round
Tears on chrome
Holding this horse's head
Visions almost dead

I suddenly fall forward!
With baby Tess
All grown

And
Everything
Said

Kiss This Heart

Kiss this heart
Tear the bones apart
Rip the flesh smart.

Don't leave
Don't dart.

Memory awake
Childhood cake
Confusion only bake.

True love
Awake!!

Young old heart
Of mine reawake!

Take me back
To my life
I'm older then than now.

My heart is kissed
Daddy attacked.

Wind of Life

Pass through me
Blow my cells
Carry away thoughts
And hell

Open the mill
Of life's overkill

Dance with me
Again

Then I'll see
You and me
Ringing life's bell
From the force of the wind

Not adversarial

Or "Mommy Dearest"

But with dear folk being kin

Do En My Laundry

Do en my laundry
At Motel 6
On Christmas morning
In Phoenix, Arizona, all sick.

But I feel so great
My daughter's a senior at Arizona State
This Dec '04
And soon will
Graduate.

Life is good
And this day is special
You see, God is a parent, too!
Baby Jesus is due.

Rebellion/Control

Rebellion, hellion
Our mother's face
We get disgrace

Control, rectification
On our own
We get direction

Rebellion, control
Flip-flop
Our goal

Except when control
Reveals itself
Hate is our soul

You see they are the same

And you are the last to know

That it's anger and fear

Giving game
And pain

Get a Grip

Life's been hard
And I took a hit,

Like a three-part song:
American Pie,
Stairway to Heaven,
Everlasting Love,
Ka dong!

Love a dog
Call a mom
Pray to God
Stop the fog!

But if all fails
Remember,

The answer to life
Keep love in sight!
Anticipate!
Give up hate,
You just might find

Your own
God-self light.

Has Been Me

Disillusionment … reality down
Box like Ali
Switch-hittin' Mantle … me.
Cocky in life and a clown.

Looking back
Gravity fed
Rainbowed
Misconnections … yak yak.

Love of psyche
Heart of gold
It's all a dream
'Cept this picture of you
That I hold.

I climb into bed
Pull up the covers
Fluff the pillow
Turn to the cool wall I wed.

Let go a great big sigh
And ask God one more time
Roll the film.

In silence I grin
And in my mind I find
I've been all that I've been …

CUT!!!

Mammal

Sea driven!
Pulled!

Reptile mist.

Warmth, and children born
Tear-duct-eye *we see*!

Long long long journey of life

No more cold prickly
But warm fuzzy me!

Holding baby,

A mother's delight, and God's destiny!

From Darwin, Einstein, Freud,
And especially Shakespeare
You know you have a heart
When your child is born—
And your heart walks the earth
Without thee.

And it cometh to be known
You loveth, someone
More than yourself
And the sea.

Lifetime

The beverage of a lifetime
Is being who you are.

The beverage of a lifetime
Is seeing near and far.

Ma and Pa
Not family law.

Being honest with yourself
Doing the right thing.

God, love, and peace of mind
Is ever so kind.

The beverage of a lifetime
Is being who you are.

Think dada
And sing!

Кристен

Spring 1995

Thank goodness and love, my …
Russian cowgirl, scholar, sigh …
Turn around, go within your eye …
The eye is upside down and lies …
Keep a vision of our love, never good-bye.

What Is the Sound of One Flip-Flop Flopping?

Flip flop flip flop
Cold hot, cold hot
Opposite caught!

What is the sound of one flip-flop flopping?

Surrender, spirit, then

Flop!!!

I love you a lot.

Because of words not said
Before dead
Is dead.

Favorite Word—Rainbow

Rainbow
Colors brilliant

In order
And perfect lines

Sunshine
And air-a-mist

And your smile
Is not missed

My heart aglow
A God vision so

The answer is not in
The rainbow arc

But the rainbow's
Heart

And in the eyes of the viewers
With all its brilliance

And mark

Brothers

Number 1 brother left   Thinks he's Superman
Number 2 brother   holiday phone call
Number 3 brother   Gypsy—left holiday message.

Shuffle the cards,
Throw the dice,
Contact with brothers
Is so "nice."

You see we came
From Mom.
    Flip-flops, shorts, and cigarette in mouth.
        She died of blood cancer
        And that wasn't so nice.

Greatest Generation/Greatest Relation

Upper and rough
    Canadian border
    Michigander
    Winter tough.

Feeding neighborhood dogs
And snowbound,
It's her beauty
Of love
All around.

To my favorite relative
Aunt Helen
My love I send.

Mom2

Eighty-year-old birthday gal
Angled push-ups
Against the table she soars
Birthday song and cake
We adore.

But it's life,
Longevity, and
Stepmom's wisdom
That's my core.

Printed in the United States
By Bookmasters